Cram101 Textbook Outlines to accompany:

Current Directions In Social Psychology

Ruscher, Hammer, 1st Edition

An Academic Internet Publishers (AIPI) publication (c) 2007.

You have a discounted membership at www.Cram101.com with this book.

Get all of the practice tests for the chapters of this textbook, and access in-depth reference material for writing essays and papers. Here is an example from a Cram101 Biology text:

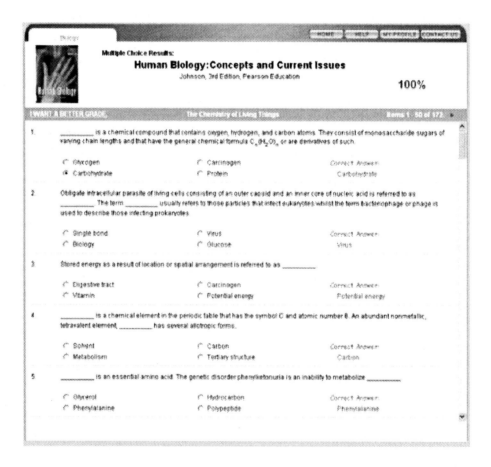

When you need problem solving help with math, stats, and other disciplines, www.Cram101.com will walk through the formulas and solutions step by step.

With Cram101.com online, you also have access to extensive reference material.

You will nail those essays and papers. Here is an example from a Cram101 Biology text:

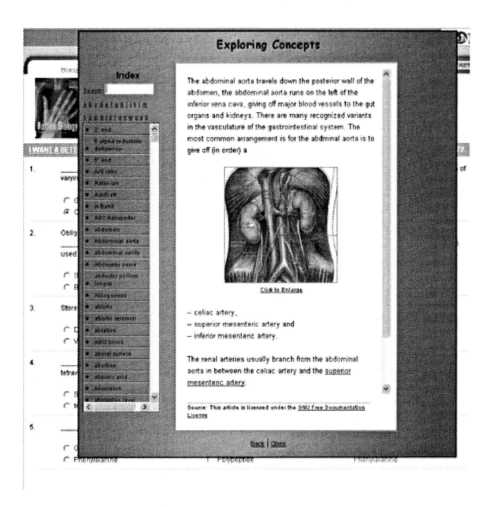

Visit **www.Cram101.com**, click Sign Up at the top of the screen, and enter DK73DW in the promo code box on the registration screen. Access to www.Cram101.com is normally $9.95, but because you have purchased this book, your access fee is only $4.95. Sign up and stop highlighting textbooks forever.

Learning System

Cram101 Textbook Outlines is a learning system. The notes in this book are the highlights of your textbook, you will never have to highlight a book again.

How to use this book. Take this book to class, it is your notebook for the lecture. The notes and highlights on the left hand side of the pages follow the outline and order of the textbook. All you have to do is follow along while your intructor presents the lecture. Circle the items emphasized in class and add other important information on the right side. With Cram101 Textbook Outlines you'll spend less time writing and more time listening. Learning becomes more efficient.

Cram101.com Online

Increase your studying efficiency by using Cram101.com's practice tests and online reference material. It is the perfect complement to Cram101 Textbook Outlines. Use self-teaching matching tests or simulate in-class testing with comprehensive multiple choice tests, or simply use Cram's true and false tests for quick review. Cram101.com even allows you to enter your in-class notes for an integrated studying format combining the textbook notes with your class notes.

Visit **www.Cram101.com**, click Sign Up at the top of the screen, and enter **DK73DW3395** in the promo code box on the registration screen. Access to www.Cram101.com is normally $9.95, but because you have purchased this book, your access fee is only $4.95. Sign up and stop highlighting textbooks forever.

Current Directions In Social Psychology
Ruscher, Hammer, 1st

CONTENTS

Social psychology	Social psychology is the study of the nature and causes of human social behavior, with an emphasis on how people think towards each other and how they relate to each other.
Social psychologists	Social psychologists study the nature and causes of human social behavior, emphasizing on how people think and relate towards each other.
Executive function	The processes involved in regulating attention and in determining what to do with information just gathered or retrieved from long-term memory, is referred to as the executive function.
Self-esteem	Self-esteem refers to a person's subjective appraisal of himself or herself as intrinsically positive or negative to some degree.
Self-affirmation theory	Self-affirmation theory suggests that people will often cope with specific threats to their self-esteem by reminding themselves of other unrelated but cherished aspects of their self-concept.
Cognitive dissonance	Cognitive dissonance is a state of opposition between cognitions. Contradicting cognitions serve as a driving force that compel the mind to acquire or invent new thoughts or beliefs, or to modify existing beliefs, so as to minimize the amount of dissonance between cognitions.
Social comparison	Social comparison theory is the idea that individuals learn about and assess themselves by comparison with other people. Research shows that individuals tend to lean more toward social comparisons in situations that are ambiguous.
Theories	Theories are logically self-consistent models or frameworks describing the behavior of a certain natural or social phenomenon. They are broad explanations and predictions concerning phenomena of interest.
Population	Population refers to all members of a well-defined group of organisms, events, or things.
Affect	A subjective feeling or emotional tone often accompanied by bodily expressions noticeable to others is called affect.
Motives	Needs or desires that energize and direct behavior toward a goal are motives.
Defense mechanism	A Defense mechanism is a set of unconscious ways to protect one's personality from unpleasant thoughts and realities which may otherwise cause anxiety. The notion is an integral part of the psychoanalytic theory.
Attention	Attention is the cognitive process of selectively concentrating on one thing while ignoring other things. Psychologists have labeled three types of attention: sustained attention, selective attention, and divided attention.
Antecedents	In behavior modification, events that typically precede the target response are called antecedents.
Aronson	Aronson is credited with refining the theory of cognitive dissonance, which posits that when attitudes and behaviors are inconsistent with one another that psychological discomfort results. This discomfort motivates the person experiencing it to either change their behavior or attitude so that consonance is restored.
Attitude	An enduring mental representation of a person, place, or thing that evokes an emotional response and related behavior is called attitude.
Questionnaire	A self-report method of data collection or clinical assessment method in which the individual being studied checks off items on a printed list, answers multiple-choice questions, or writes out answers to essay questions aimed at producing a selfdescription is called questionnaire.
Motivation	In psychology, motivation is the driving force (desire) behind all actions of an organism.
Control subjects	Control subjects are participants in an experiment who do not receive the treatment effect but for whom all other conditions are held comparable to those of experimental subjects.

Go to **Cram101.com** for the Practice Tests for this Chapter.

Creativity	Creativity is the ability to think about something in novel and unusual ways and come up with unique solutions to problems. It involves divergent thinking, having many solutions or views to a problem.
Feedback	Feedback refers to information returned to a person about the effects a response has had.
American Psychological Association	The American Psychological Association is a professional organization representing psychology in the US. The mission statement is to "advance psychology as a science and profession and as a means of promoting health, education , and human welfare".
Personality	Personality refers to the pattern of enduring characteristics that differentiates a person, the patterns of behaviors that make each individual unique.
Hypocrisy	Publicly advocating some attitude or behavior and then acting in a way that is inconsistent with this espoused attitude or behavior is called hypocrisy.
Cognition	The intellectual processes through which information is obtained, transformed, stored, retrieved, and otherwise used is cognition.
Variable	A variable refers to a measurable factor, characteristic, or attribute of an individual or a system.
Assimilation	According to Piaget, assimilation is the process of the organism interacting with the environment given the organism's cognitive structure. Assimilation is reuse of schemas to fit new information.
Social influence	Social influence is when the actions or thoughts of individual(s) are changed by other individual(s). Peer pressure is an example of social influence.
Self-concept	Self-concept refers to domain-specific evaluations of the self where a domain may be academics, athletics, etc.
Perception	Perception is the process of acquiring, interpreting, selecting, and organizing sensory information.
Theory of social comparison	The theory of social comparison suggests that people look to others for cues about how to behave when they are in confusing or unfamiliar situation.
Festinger	The theory of social comparison processes, developed by Festinger, suggests that there are large areas of judgment in which reality depends on consensus; it is socially defined. He also developed the cognitive dissonance theory: cognitions that are not in harmony act like drives, motivating actions to resolve dissonance.
Hypothesis	A specific statement about behavior or mental processes that is testable through research is a hypothesis.
Attribution theory	Attribution theory is concerned with the ways in which people explain the behavior of others. It explores how individuals "attribute" causes to events and how this cognitive perception affects their motivation.
Cognitive psychology	Cognitive psychology is the psychological science which studies the mental processes that are hypothesised to underlie behavior. This covers a broad range of research domains, examining questions about the workings of memory, attention, perception, knowledge representation, reasoning, creativity and problem solving.
Social cognition	Social cognition is the name for both a branch of psychology that studies the cognitive processes involved in social interaction, and an umbrella term for the processes themselves. It uses the tools and assumptions of cognitive psychology to study how people understand themselves and others in society and social situations.
Insight	Insight refers to a sudden awareness of the relationships among various elements that had previously appeared to be independent of one another.
Emotion	An emotion is a mental states that arise spontaneously, rather than through conscious effort. They are often accompanied by physiological changes.

Clinical psychologist	A psychologist, usually with a Ph.D, whose training is in the diagnosis, treatment, or research of psychological and behavioral disorders is a clinical psychologist.
Baseline	Measure of a particular behavior or process taken before the introduction of the independent variable or treatment is called the baseline.
Role model	A person who serves as a positive example of desirable behavior is referred to as a role model.
Affective	Affective is the way people react emotionally, their ability to feel another living thing's pain or
Anchor	An anchor is a sample of work or performance used to set the specific performance standard for a rubric level .
Construct	A generalized concept, such as anxiety or gravity, is a construct.
Reasoning	Reasoning is the act of using reason to derive a conclusion from certain premises. There are two main methods to reach a conclusion,deductive reasoning and inductive reasoning.
Learning	Learning is a relatively permanent change in behavior that results from experience. Thus, to attribute a behavioral change to learning, the change must be relatively permanent and must result from experience.
Self-image	A person's self-image is the mental picture, generally of a kind that is quite resistant to change, that depicts not only details that are potentially available to objective investigation by others, but also items that have been learned by that person about himself or herself.
Social policy	Social policy is the study of the welfare state, and the range of responses to social need.
Empirical	Empirical means the use of working hypotheses which are capable of being disproved using observation or experiment.
Downward social comparison	The defensive tendency to compare ourselves with others who are worse off than we are is called downward social comparison.
Critical thinking	Critical thinking is a mental process of analyzing or evaluating information, particularly statements or propositions that are offered as true.
Illusion	An illusion is a distortion of a sensory perception.
Egocentrism	The inability to distinguish between one's own perspective and someone else's is referred to as egocentrism.
Variability	Statistically, variability refers to how much the scores in a distribution spread out, away from the mean.
Phenomenology	Phenomenology is the study of subjective mental experiences; a theme of humanistic theories of personality. It studies meaningful, intact mental events without dividing them for further analysis.
Kahneman	Kahneman is famous for collaboration with Amos Tversky and others in establishing a cognitive basis for common human errors using heuristics and in developing prospect theory.
Habituation	In habituation there is a progressive reduction in the response probability with continued repetition of a stimulus.
Anchoring and adjustment	Anchoring and adjustment is a psychological heuristic said to influence the way people estimate probabilities intuitively. According to this heuristic, people start with an implicitly suggested reference point and make adjustments to it to reach their estimate.
Anagram	An anagram is a type of word play, the result of rearranging the letters of a word or phrase to produce other words, using all the original letters exactly once.
Acute	Acute means sudden, sharp, and abrupt. Usually short in duration.
Sensation	Sensation is the first stage in the chain of biochemical and neurologic events that begins with the

impinging of a stimulus upon the receptor cells of a sensory organ, which then leads to perception, the mental state that is reflected in statements like "I see a uniformly blue wall."

Paradigm	Paradigm refers to the set of practices that defines a scientific discipline during a particular period of time. It provides a framework from which to conduct research, it ensures that a certain range of phenomena, those on which the paradigm focuses, are explored thoroughly. Itmay also blind scientists to other, perhaps more fruitful, ways of dealing with their subject matter.
Intuition	Quick, impulsive thought that does not make use of formal logic or clear reasoning is referred to as intuition.
Inference	Inference is the act or process of drawing a conclusion based solely on what one already knows.
Anchoring	Anchoring or focalism is a term used in psychology to describe the common human tendency to rely too heavily, or "anchor," on one trait or piece of information when making decisions.
Script	A schema, or behavioral sequence, for an event is called a script. It is a form of schematic organization, with real-world events organized in terms of temporal and causal relations between component acts.
Egocentric bias	Egocentric bias occurs when people claim more responsibility for themselves for the results of a joint action than an outside observer would.
Guilt	Guilt describes many concepts related to a negative emotion or condition caused by actions which are believed to be, morally wrong. According to Freud, the avoidance of guilt is the basis for moral behavior.
Society	The social sciences use the term society to mean a group of people that form a semi-closed (or semi-open) social system, in which most interactions are with other individuals belonging to the group.
Stages	Stages represent relatively discrete periods of time in which functioning is qualitatively different from functioning at other periods.
Syndrome	The term syndrome is the association of several clinically recognizable features, signs, symptoms, phenomena or characteristics which often occur together, so that the presence of one feature indicates the presence of the others.
Social support	Social Support is the physical and emotional comfort given by family, friends, co-workers and others. Research has identified three main types of social support: emotional, practical, sharing points of view.
Self-efficacy	Self-efficacy is the belief that one has the capabilities to execute the courses of actions required to manage prospective situations.
Eating disorders	Psychological disorders characterized by distortion of the body image and gross disturbances in eating patterns are called eating disorders.
Etiology	Etiology is the study of causation. The term is used in philosophy, physics and biology in reference to the causes of various phenomena. It is generally the study of why things occur, or even the reasons behind the way that things act.
Binge	Binge refers to relatively brief episode of uncontrolled, excessive consumption.
Ego	In Freud's view the Ego serves to balance our primitive needs and our moral beliefs and taboos. Relying on experience, a healthy Ego provides the ability to adapt to reality and interact with the outside world.
Health psychology	The field of psychology that studies the relationships between psychological factors and the prevention and treatment of physical illness is called health psychology.
Planning fallacy	The planning fallacy is the tendency to underestimate task-completion times.

Ideology	An ideology can be thought of as a comprehensive vision, as a way of looking at things, as in common sense and several philosophical tendencies, or a set of ideas proposed by the dominant class of a society to all members of this society.
Obesity	The state of being more than 20 percent above the average weight for a person of one's height is called obesity.
Clinical psychology	Clinical psychology is involved in the diagnosis, assessment, and treatment of patients with mental or behavioral disorders, and conducts research in these various areas.
Psychotherapy	Psychotherapy is a set of techniques based on psychological principles intended to improve mental health, emotional or behavioral issues.

Go to **Cram101.com** for the Practice Tests for this Chapter.

Stereotype	A stereotype is considered to be a group concept, held by one social group about another. They are often used in a negative or prejudicial sense and are frequently used to justify certain discriminatory behaviors. This allows powerful social groups to legitimize and protect their dominant position
Mere exposure effect	The mere exposure effect is a psychological artifact well known to advertisers: people express undue liking for things merely because they are familiar with them. This effect has been nicknamed the "familiarity breeds liking" effect.
Zajonc	Zajonc is best known for his decades of work on the mere exposure effect, the phenomenon that repeated exposure to a stimulus brings about an attitude change in relation to the stimulus.
Adaptation	Adaptation is a lowering of sensitivity to a stimulus following prolonged exposure to that stimulus. Behavioral adaptations are special ways a particular organism behaves to survive in its natural habitat.
Gene	A gene is an ultramicroscopic area of the chromosome. It is the smallest physical unit of the DNA molecule that carries a piece of hereditary information.
Affective	Affective is the way people react emotionally, their ability to feel another living thing's pain or joy.
Brain	The brain controls and coordinates most movement, behavior and homeostatic body functions such as heartbeat, blood pressure, fluid balance and body temperature. Functions of the brain are responsible for cognition, emotion, memory, motor learning and other sorts of learning. The brain is primarily made up of two types of cells: glia and neurons.
Species	Species refers to a reproductively isolated breeding population.
Emotion	An emotion is a mental states that arise spontaneously, rather than through conscious effort. They are often accompanied by physiological changes.
Display rules	Sociocultural standards that determine when, where, and how emotions should be expressed are called display rules.
Dispositional causes	Perceived causes of behavior that are based on internal traits or personality factors are dispositional causes.
Fundamental attribution error	The fundamental attribution error is the tendency for people to over-emphasize dispositional, or personality-based, explanations for behaviors observed in others while under-emphasizing the role and power of situational influences on the same behavior.
Personality	Personality refers to the pattern of enduring characteristics that differentiates a person, the patterns of behaviors that make each individual unique.
Evolution	Commonly used to refer to gradual change, evolution is the change in the frequency of alleles within a population from one generation to the next. This change may be caused by different mechanisms, including natural selection, genetic drift, or changes in population (gene flow).
Decoding	Process of phonetic analysis by which a printed word is converted to spoken form before retrieval from long-term memory is called decoding.
Stimulus	A change in an environmental condition that elicits a response is a stimulus.
Paradigm	Paradigm refers to the set of practices that defines a scientific discipline during a particular period of time. It provides a framework from which to conduct research, it ensures that a certain range of phenomena, those on which the paradigm focuses, are explored thoroughly. Itmay also blind scientists to other, perhaps more fruitful, ways of dealing with their subject matter.
Classical	Classical conditioning is a simple form of learning in which an organism comes to associate

Go to **Cram101.com** for the Practice Tests for this Chapter.

conditioning	or anticipate events. A neutral stimulus comes to evoke the response usually evoked by a natural or unconditioned stimulus by being paired repeatedly with the unconditioned stimulus.
Unconditioned stimulus	In classical conditioning, an unconditioned stimulus elicits a response from an organism prior to conditioning. It is a naturally occurring stimulus and a naturally occurring response..
Empirical	Empirical means the use of working hypotheses which are capable of being disproved using observation or experiment.
Affect	A subjective feeling or emotional tone often accompanied by bodily expressions noticeable to others is called affect.
Operant Conditioning	A simple form of learning in which an organism learns to engage in behavior because it is reinforced is referred to as operant conditioning. The consequences of a behavior produce changes in the probability of the behavior's occurence.
Conformity	Conformity is the degree to which members of a group will change their behavior, views and attitudes to fit the views of the group. The group can influence members via unconscious processes or via overt social pressure on individuals.
Sensory receptor	A sensory receptor is a structure that recognizes a stimulus in the environment of an organism. In response to stimuli the sensory receptor initiates sensory transduction by creating graded potentials or action potentials in the same cell or in an adjacent one.
Negative Reinforcement	During negative reinforcement, a stimulus is removed and the frequency of the behavior or response increases.
Random sample	A sample drawn so that each member of a population has an equal chance of being selected to participate is referred to as a random sample.
Correlation	A statistical technique for determining the degree of association between two or more variables is referred to as correlation.
Valence	In expectancy theory, the value or worth a person gives to an outcome is called the valence.
Titchener	Titchener attempted to classify the structures of the mind, not unlike the way a chemist breaks down chemicals into their component parts-water into hydrogen and oxygen for example. He conceived of hydrogen and oxygen as structures of a chemical compound, and sensations and thoughts as structures of the mind. This approach became known as structuralism.
Conditioning	Conditioning describes the process by which behaviors can be learned or modified through interaction with the environment.
Conditioned stimulus	A previously neutral stimulus that elicits the conditioned response because of being repeatedly paired with a stimulus that naturally elicited that response, is called a conditioned stimulus.
Unconditioned response	An Unconditioned Response is the response elicited to an unconditioned stimulus. It is a natural, automatic response.
Innate	Innate behavior is not learned or influenced by the environment, rather, it is present or predisposed at birth.
Conditioned response	A conditioned response is the response to a stimulus that occurs when an animal has learned to associate the stimulus with a certain positive or negative effect.
Imprinting	Imprinting describes any kind of critical period sensitive learning (learning occurring at a particular age or a particular life stage) that is rapid and apparently independent of the consequences of behavior.
Cognitive	Lazarus' term for individuals' interpretation of events in their lives as threatening,

Go to **Cram101.com** for the Practice Tests for this Chapter.

appraisal	harmful, or challenging and their determination of whether they have the resources to effectively cope with the events is referred to as cognitive appraisal.
Recognition memory	An ability to correctly identify previously learned information is recognition memory.
Cognition	The intellectual processes through which information is obtained, transformed, stored, retrieved, and otherwise used is cognition.
Hypothesis	A specific statement about behavior or mental processes that is testable through research is a hypothesis.
Hippocampus	The hippocampus is a part of the brain located inside the temporal lobe. It forms a part of the limbic system and plays a part in memory and navigation.
Amygdala	Located in the brain's medial temporal lobe, the almond-shaped amygdala is believed to play a key role in the emotions. It forms part of the limbic system and is linked to both fear responses and pleasure. Its size is positively correlated with aggressive behavior across species.
Lesion	A lesion is a non-specific term referring to abnormal tissue in the body. It can be caused by any disease process including trauma (physical, chemical, electrical), infection, neoplasm, metabolic and autoimmune.
Homogeneous	In biology homogeneous has a meaning similar to its meaning in mathematics. Generally it means "the same" or "of the same quality or general property".
Mere-exposure effect	The mere-exposure effect is the tendency of some people to develop a more positive evaluation of some person, object, or other stimulus simply with repeated exposure.
Attachment	Attachment is the tendency to seek closeness to another person and feel secure when that person is present.
Generalizability	The ability to extend a set of findings observed in one piece of research to other situations and groups is called generalizability.
Social psychology	Social psychology is the study of the nature and causes of human social behavior, with an emphasis on how people think towards each other and how they relate to each other.
Experimental psychology	Experimental psychology is an approach to psychology that treats it as one of the natural sciences, and therefore assumes that it is susceptible to the experimental method.
Learning	Learning is a relatively permanent change in behavior that results from experience. Thus, to attribute a behavioral change to learning, the change must be relatively permanent and must result from experience.
Discrimination	In Learning theory, discrimination refers the ability to distinguish between a conditioned stimulus and other stimuli. It can be brought about by extensive training or differential reinforcement. In social terms, it is the denial of privileges to a person or a group on the basis of prejudice.
Neuroscience	A field that combines the work of psychologists, biologists, biochemists, medical researchers, and others in the study of the structure and function of the nervous system is neuroscience.
Survey	A method of scientific investigation in which a large sample of people answer questions about their attitudes or behavior is referred to as a survey.
Priming	A phenomenon in which exposure to a word or concept later makes it easier to recall related information, even when one has no conscious memory of the word or concept is called priming.
Postnatal	Postnatal is the period beginning immediately after the birth of a child and extending for

	about six weeks. The period is also known as postpartum and, less commonly, puerperium.
Prenatal	Prenatal period refers to the time from conception to birth.
Inference	Inference is the act or process of drawing a conclusion based solely on what one already knows.
Social cognition	Social cognition is the name for both a branch of psychology that studies the cognitive processes involved in social interaction, and an umbrella term for the processes themselves. It uses the tools and assumptions of cognitive psychology to study how people understand themselves and others in society and social situations.
Automaticity	The ability to process information with little or no effort is referred to as automaticity.
Attention	Attention is the cognitive process of selectively concentrating on one thing while ignoring other things. Psychologists have labeled three types of attention: sustained attention, selective attention, and divided attention.
Brain-imaging	Brain-imaging is a fairly recent discipline within medicine and neuroscience. Brain imaging falls into two broad categories -- structural imaging and functional imaging.
Pupil	In the eye, the pupil is the opening in the middle of the iris. It appears black because most of the light entering it is absorbed by the tissues inside the eye. The size of the pupil is controlled by involuntary contraction and dilation of the iris, in order to regulate the intensity of light entering the eye. This is known as the pupillary reflex.
Darwin	Darwin achieved lasting fame as originator of the theory of evolution through natural selection. His book Expression of Emotions in Man and Animals is generally considered the first text on comparative psychology.
Evolutionary perspective	A perspective that focuses on how humans have evolved and adapted behaviors required for survival against various environmental pressures over the long course is called the evolutionary perspective.
Electromyography	Electromyography is a medical technique for measuring muscle response to nervous stimulation.
Autonomic nervous system	A division of the peripheral nervous system, the autonomic nervous system, regulates glands and activities such as heartbeat, respiration, digestion, and dilation of the pupils. It is responsible for homeostasis, maintaining a relatively constant internal environment .
Perception	Perception is the process of acquiring, interpreting, selecting, and organizing sensory information.
Temporal lobe	The temporal lobe is part of the cerebrum. It lies at the side of the brain, beneath the lateral or Sylvian fissure. Adjacent areas in the superior, posterior and lateral parts of the temporal lobe are involved in high-level auditory processing.
Social information processing	The view that social information must be encoded, compared with other pertinent information, and retrieved so that social interactions run smoothly is called social information processing.
Cerebral cortex	The cerebral cortex is the outermost layer of the cerebrum and has a grey color. It is made up of four lobes and it is involved in many complex brain functions including memory, perceptual awareness, "thinking", language and consciousness. The cerebral cortex receives sensory information from many different sensory organs eg: eyes, ears, etc. and processes the information.
Normative	The term normative is used to describe the effects of those structures of culture which regulate the function of social activity.
Functional	Functional Magnetic Resonance Imaging describes the use of MRI to measure hemodynamic signals

Go to **Cram101.com** for the Practice Tests for this Chapter.

magnetic resonance imaging	related to neural activity in the brain or spinal cord of humans or other animals. It is one of the most recently developed forms of brain imaging.
Positron emission tomography	Positron Emission Tomography measures emissions from radioactively labeled chemicals that have been injected into the bloodstream. The greatest benefit is that different compounds can show blood flow and oxygen and glucose metabolism in the tissues of the working brain.
Midbrain	Located between the hindbrain and forebrain, a region in which many nerve-fiber systems ascend and descend to connect the higher and lower portions of the brain is referred to as midbrain. It is archipallian in origin, meaning its general architecture is shared with the most ancient of vertebrates. Dopamine produced in the subtantia nigra plays a role in motivation and habituation of species from humans to the most elementary animals such as insects.
Thalamus	An area near the center of the brain involved in the relay of sensory information to the cortex and in the functions of sleep and attention is the thalamus.
Basic emotions	Basic emotions are those found in all cultures, as evidinced by the same facial expressions. They include: fear, anger, disgust, surprise, happiness, and distress.
Motivation	In psychology, motivation is the driving force (desire) behind all actions of an organism.
Preparedness	The species-specific biological predisposition to learn in certain ways is called preparedness.
Phobia	A persistent, irrational fear of an object, situation, or activity that the person feels compelled to avoid is referred to as a phobia.
Functional analysis	A systematic study of behavior in which one identifies the stimuli that trigger the behavior and the reinforcers that maintain it is a functional analysis. Relations between the two become the cause-and-effect relationships in behavior and are the laws of a science. A synthesis of these various laws expressed in quantitative terms yields a comprehensive picture of the organism as a behaving system without postulating internal processes.
Associative learning	A metal connection made between two events is called associative learning.
Pavlov	Pavlov first described the phenomenon now known as classical conditioning in experiments with dogs.
Neuroimaging	Neuroimaging comprises all invasive, minimally invasive, and non-invasive methods for obtaining structural and functional images of the nervous system's major subsystems: the brain, the peripheral nervous system, and the spinal cord.
Ekman	Ekman found that at least some facial expressions and their corresponding emotions are not culturally determined, and thus presumably biological in origin. Expressions he found to be universal included anger, disgust, fear, joy, sadness and surprise.
Cross-cultural studies	Cross-cultural studies are comparisons of a culture with one or more other cultures, which provides information about the degree to which behavior is similar across cultures or the degree to which it is culture specific .
Meta-analysis	In statistics, a meta-analysis combines the results of several studies that address a set of related research hypotheses.
Norms	In testing, standards of test performance that permit the comparison of one person's score on the test to the scores of others who have taken the same test are referred to as norms.
Universal grammar	Chomsky's theory that all the world's languages share a similar underlying structure is called universal grammar. It attempts to explain language acquisition in general, not

describe specific languages.

Metaphor	A metaphor is a rhetorical trope where a comparison is made between two seemingly unrelated subjects
Empirical evidence	Facts or information based on direct observation or experience are referred to as empirical evidence.
Nurture	Nurture refers to the environmental influences on behavior due to nutrition, culture, socioeconomic status, and learning.
Guilford	Guilford observed that most individuals display a preference for either convergent or divergent thinking. Scientists and engineers typically prefer the former and artists and performers, the latter.
Reasoning	Reasoning is the act of using reason to derive a conclusion from certain premises. There are two main methods to reach a conclusion,deductive reasoning and inductive reasoning.
Cognitive science	Cognitive Science is the scientific study of the mind and brain and how they give rise to behavior. The field is highly interdisciplinary and is closely related to several other areas, including psychology, artificial intelligence, linguistics and psycholinguistics, philosophy, neuroscience, logic, robotics, anthropology and biology.
Marijuana	Marijuana is the dried vegetable matter of the Cannabis sativa plant. It contains large concentrations of compounds that have medicinal and psychoactive effects when consumed, usually by smoking or eating.
Pedagogy	Pedagogy is the art or science of teaching. The word comes from the ancient Greek paidagogos, the slave who took children to and from school.
Population	Population refers to all members of a well-defined group of organisms, events, or things.
Theories	Theories are logically self-consistent models or frameworks describing the behavior of a certain natural or social phenomenon. They are broad explanations and predictions concerning phenomena of interest.
Moral character	Moral character or character is an abstract evaluation of a person's moral and mental qualities. Such an evaluation is subjective — one person may evaluate someone's character on the basis of their virtue, another may consider their fortitude, courage, loyalty, honesty, or piety.
Trait	An enduring personality characteristic that tends to lead to certain behaviors is called a trait. The term trait also means a genetically inherited feature of an organism.
Ethnography	Ethnography is a holistic research method founded in the idea that a system's properties cannot necessarily be accurately understood independently of each other.
Aristotle	Aristotle can be credited with the development of the first theory of learning. He concluded that ideas were generated in consciousness based on four principlesof association: contiguity, similarity, contrast, and succession. In contrast to Plato, he believed that knowledge derived from sensory experience and was not inherited.
Socioeconomic Status	A family's socioeconomic status is based on family income, parental education level, parental occupation, and social status in the community. Those with high status often have more success in preparing their children for school because they have access to a wide range of resources.
Demographic variable	A varying characteristic that is a vital or social statistic of an individual, sample group, or population, for example, age, sex, socioeconomic status, racial origin, education is called a demographic variable.

Collectivist	A person who defines the self in terms of relationships to other people and groups and gives priority to group goals is called collectivist.
Individualism	Individualism refers to putting personal goals ahead of group goals and defining one's identity in terms of personal attributes rather than group memberships.
Individualist	A person who defines the self in terms of personal traits and gives priority to personal goals is an individualist.
Ethnic group	An ethnic group is a culture or subculture whose members are readily distinguishable by outsiders based on traits originating from a common racial, national, linguistic, or religious source. Members of an ethnic group are often presumed to be culturally or biologically similar, although this is not in fact necessarily the case.
Individual differences	Individual differences psychology studies the ways in which individual people differ in their behavior. This is distinguished from other aspects of psychology in that although psychology is ostensibly a study of individuals, modern psychologists invariably study groups.
Attitude	An enduring mental representation of a person, place, or thing that evokes an emotional response and related behavior is called attitude.
Critical thinking	Critical thinking is a mental process of analyzing or evaluating information, particularly statements or propositions that are offered as true.

Insight	Insight refers to a sudden awareness of the relationships among various elements that had previously appeared to be independent of one another.
Attention	Attention is the cognitive process of selectively concentrating on one thing while ignoring other things. Psychologists have labeled three types of attention: sustained attention, selective attention, and divided attention.
Ethnic group	An ethnic group is a culture or subculture whose members are readily distinguishable by outsiders based on traits originating from a common racial, national, linguistic, or religious source. Members of an ethnic group are often presumed to be culturally or biologically similar, although this is not in fact necessarily the case.
Social psychologists	Social psychologists study the nature and causes of human social behavior, emphasizing on how people think and relate towards each other.
Laboratory setting	Research setting in which the behavior of interest does not naturally occur is called a laboratory setting.
Depression	In everyday language depression refers to any downturn in mood, which may be relatively transitory and perhaps due to something trivial. This is differentiated from Clinical depression which is marked by symptoms that last two weeks or more and are so severe that they interfere with daily living.
Adolescence	The period of life bounded by puberty and the assumption of adult responsibilities is adolescence.
Gender difference	A gender difference is a disparity between genders involving quality or quantity. Though some gender differences are controversial, they are not to be confused with sexist stereotypes.
Evolution	Commonly used to refer to gradual change, evolution is the change in the frequency of alleles within a population from one generation to the next. This change may be caused by different mechanisms, including natural selection, genetic drift, or changes in population (gene flow).
Fetus	A fetus develops from the end of the 8th week of pregnancy (when the major structures have formed), until birth.
Gene	A gene is an ultramicroscopic area of the chromosome. It is the smallest physical unit of the DNA molecule that carries a piece of hereditary information.
Individual differences	Individual differences psychology studies the ways in which individual people differ in their behavior. This is distinguished from other aspects of psychology in that although psychology is ostensibly a study of individuals, modern psychologists invariably study groups.
Attachment style	Attachment style refers to the way a person typically interacts with significant others.
Social support	Social Support is the physical and emotional comfort given by family, friends, co-workers and others. Research has identified three main types of social support: emotional, practical, sharing points of view.
Perception	Perception is the process of acquiring, interpreting, selecting, and organizing sensory information.
Hypothesis	A specific statement about behavior or mental processes that is testable through research is a hypothesis.
Motives	Needs or desires that energize and direct behavior toward a goal are motives.
Information processing	Information processing is an approach to the goal of understanding human thinking. The essence of the approach is to see cognition as being essentially computational in nature, with mind being the software and the brain being the hardware.
Empirical	Facts or information based on direct observation or experience are referred to as empirical

evidence	evidence.
Postulates	Postulates are general statements about behavior that cannot be directly verified. They are used to generate theorems which can be tested.
Factor analysis	Factor analysis is a statistical technique that originated in psychometrics. The objective is to explain the most of the variability among a number of observable random variables in terms of a smaller number of unobservable random variables called factors.
Reliability	Reliability means the extent to which a test produces a consistent , reproducible score .
Validity	The extent to which a test measures what it is intended to measure is called validity.
Longitudinal study	Longitudinal study is a type of developmental study in which the same group of participants is followed and measured for an extended period of time, often years.
Paradoxical	Paradoxical intention refers to instructing clients to do the opposite of the desired behavior. Telling an impotent man not to have sex or an insomniac not to sleep reduces anxiety to perform.
Theories	Theories are logically self-consistent models or frameworks describing the behavior of a certain natural or social phenomenon. They are broad explanations and predictions concerning phenomena of interest.
Social psychology	Social psychology is the study of the nature and causes of human social behavior, with an emphasis on how people think towards each other and how they relate to each other.
Personality	Personality refers to the pattern of enduring characteristics that differentiates a person, the patterns of behaviors that make each individual unique.
Pluralism	Pluralism refers to the coexistence of distinct ethnic and cultural groups in the same society. Individuals with a pluralistic stance usually advocate that cultural differences be maintained and appreciated.
Critical thinking	Critical thinking is a mental process of analyzing or evaluating information, particularly statements or propositions that are offered as true.
Social motives	Social motives refer to drives acquired through experience and interaction with others.
Friendship	The essentials of friendship are reciprocity and commitment between individuals who see themselves more or less as equals. Interaction between friends rests on a more equal power base than the interaction between children and adults.
Attachment	Attachment is the tendency to seek closeness to another person and feel secure when that person is present.
Empirical	Empirical means the use of working hypotheses which are capable of being disproved using observation or experiment.
Lesbian	A lesbian is a homosexual woman. They are women who are sexually and romantically attracted to other women.
Affect	A subjective feeling or emotional tone often accompanied by bodily expressions noticeable to others is called affect.
Sexually Transmitted Disease	Sexually transmitted disease is commonly transmitted between partners through some form of sexual activity, most commonly vaginal intercourse, oral sex, or anal sex.
Sexual abuse	Sexual abuse is a term used to describe non- consentual sexual relations between two or more parties which are considered criminally and/or morally offensive.
Sexual	Sexual orientation refers to the sex or gender of people who are the focus of a person's

orientation	amorous or erotic desires, fantasies, and spontaneous feelings, the gender(s) toward which one is primarily "oriented".
Homosexual	Homosexual refers to a sexual orientation characterized by aesthetic attraction, romantic love, and sexual desire exclusively for members of the same sex or gender identity.
Late adolescence	Late adolescence refers to approximately the latter half of the second decade of life. Career interests, dating, and identity exploration are often more pronounced in late adolescence than in early adolescence.
Early adulthood	The developmental period beginning in the late teens or early twenties and lasting into the thirties is called early adulthood; characterized by an increasing self-awareness.
Quantitative	A quantitative property is one that exists in a range of magnitudes, and can therefore be measured. Measurements of any particular quantitative property are expressed as as a specific quantity, referred to as a unit, multiplied by a number.
Questionnaire	A self-report method of data collection or clinical assessment method in which the individual being studied checks off items on a printed list, answers multiple-choice questions, or writes out answers to essay questions aimed at producing a selfdescription is called questionnaire.
Developmental psychology	The branch of psychology that studies the patterns of growth and change occurring throughout life is referred to as developmental psychology.
Child development	Scientific study of the processes of change from conception through adolescence is called child development.
Major depressive disorder	The diagnosis of a major depressive disorder occurs when an individual experiences a major depressive episode and depressed characteristics, such as lethargy and depression, last for 2 weeks or longer and daily functioning becomes impaired.
Abnormal psychology	The scientific study whose objectives are to describe, explain, predict, and control behaviors that are considered strange or unusual is referred to as abnormal psychology.
Scientific research	Research that is objective, systematic, and testable is called scientific research.
Plasticity	The capacity for modification and change is referred to as plasticity.
Subjective experience	Subjective experience refers to reality as it is perceived and interpreted, not as it exists objectively.
Life span	Life span refers to the upper boundary of life, the maximum number of years an individual can live. The maximum life span of human beings is about 120 years of age. Females live an average of 6 years longer than males.
Masturbation	Masturbation is the manual excitation of the sexual organs, most often to the point of orgasm. It can refer to excitation either by oneself or by another, but commonly refers to such activities performed alone.
Effect size	An effect size is the strength or magnitude of the difference between two sets of data or, in outcome studies, between two time points for the same population. (The degree to which the null hypothesis is false).
Attitude	An enduring mental representation of a person, place, or thing that evokes an emotional response and related behavior is called attitude.
Self-concept	Self-concept refers to domain-specific evaluations of the self where a domain may be academics, athletics, etc.
Stages	Stages represent relatively discrete periods of time in which functioning is qualitatively

different from functioning at other periods.

Rape	Rape is a crime where the victim is forced into sexual activity, in particular sexual penetration, against his or her will.
Acquaintance rape	Acquaintance rape refers to non-consensual sexual activity between people who are already acquainted, or who know each other socially - friends, acquaintances, people on a date, or even people in an existing romantic relationship, where it is alleged that consent for sexual activity was not given, or was given under duress.
Variability	Statistically, variability refers to how much the scores in a distribution spread out, away from the mean.
Generalizability	The ability to extend a set of findings observed in one piece of research to other situations and groups is called generalizability.
Population	Population refers to all members of a well-defined group of organisms, events, or things.
Intrinsic motivation	Intrinsic motivation causes people to engage in an activity for its own sake. They are subjective factors and include self-determination, curiosity, challenge, effort, and others.
Paradigm	Paradigm refers to the set of practices that defines a scientific discipline during a particular period of time. It provides a framework from which to conduct research, it ensures that a certain range of phenomena, those on which the paradigm focuses, are explored thoroughly. Itmay also blind scientists to other, perhaps more fruitful, ways of dealing with their subject matter.
Shaping	The concept of reinforcing successive, increasingly accurate approximations to a target behavior is called shaping. The target behavior is broken down into a hierarchy of elemental steps, each step more sophisticated then the last. By successively reinforcing each of the the elemental steps, a form of differential reinforcement, until that step is learned while extinguishing the step below, the target behavior is gradually achieved.
Sexual dysfunction	Sexual dysfunction or sexual malfunction is difficulty during any stage of the sexual act (which includes desire, arousal, orgasm, and resolution) that prevents the individual or couple from enjoying sexual activity.
Diagnostic and Statistical Manual of Mental Disorders	The Diagnostic and Statistical Manual of Mental Disorders, published by the American Psychiatric Association, is the handbook used most often in diagnosing mental disorders in the United States and internationally.
Masters and Johnson	Masters and Johnson produced the four stage model of sexual response, which they described as the human sexual response cycle. They defined the four stages of this cycle as: excitement phase, plateau phase, orgasm, and resolution phase.
Clinical assessment	A clinical assessment is a systematic evaluation and measurement of psychological, biological, and social factors in a person presenting with a possible psychological disorder.
Meta-analysis	In statistics, a meta-analysis combines the results of several studies that address a set of related research hypotheses.
American Psychological Association	The American Psychological Association is a professional organization representing psychology in the US. The mission statement is to "advance psychology as a science and profession and as a means of promoting health, education , and human welfare".
Tolman	Tolman coined the term "cognitive map", which was an internal perceptual representation of external environmental features and landmarks. He is virtually the only behaviorist who found the Stimulus-Response theory unacceptable, because reinforcement was not necessary for

learning to occur. He felt behavior was holistic, purposive, and cognitive.

Ecological niche	Ecological niche is a term describing the relational position of a species or population in an ecosystem. More formally, it includes how a population responds to the abundance of its resources and enemies and how it affects those same factors.
Chronic	Chronic refers to a relatively long duration, usually more than a few months.
Verbal Behavior	Verbal Behavior is a book written by B.F. Skinner in which the author presents his ideas on language. For Skinner, speech, along with other forms of communication, was simply a behavior. Skinner argued that each act of speech is an inevitable consequence of the speaker's current environment and his behavioral and sensory history.
Emotion	An emotion is a mental states that arise spontaneously, rather than through conscious effort. They are often accompanied by physiological changes.
Reflection	Reflection is the process of rephrasing or repeating thoughts and feelings expressed, making the person more aware of what they are saying or thinking.
Longitudinal research	Research that studies the same subjects over an extended period of time, usually several years or more, is called longitudinal research.
Reciprocity	Reciprocity, in interpersonal attraction, is the tendency to return feelings and attitudes that are expressed about us.
Clinical psychology	Clinical psychology is involved in the diagnosis, assessment, and treatment of patients with mental or behavioral disorders, and conducts research in these various areas.
Research method	The scope of the research method is to produce some new knowledge. This, in principle, can take three main forms: Exploratory research; Constructive research; and Empirical research.

Species	Species refers to a reproductively isolated breeding population.
Gene	A gene is an ultramicroscopic area of the chromosome. It is the smallest physical unit of the DNA molecule that carries a piece of hereditary information.
Inclusive fitness	Inclusive fitness is the sum of an individual's own reproductive success plus the effects the organism has on the reproductive success of related others.
Social learning	Social learning is learning that occurs as a function of observing, retaining and replicating behavior observed in others. Although social learning can occur at any stage in life, it is thought to be particularly important during childhood, particularly as authority becomes important.
Society	The social sciences use the term society to mean a group of people that form a semi-closed (or semi-open) social system, in which most interactions are with other individuals belonging to the group.
Theories	Theories are logically self-consistent models or frameworks describing the behavior of a certain natural or social phenomenon. They are broad explanations and predictions concerning phenomena of interest.
Motivation	In psychology, motivation is the driving force (desire) behind all actions of an organism.
Death instinct	The death instinct was defined by Sigmund Freud, in Beyond the Pleasure Principle(1920). It speculated on the existence of a fundamental death wish or death instinct, referring to an individual's own need to die.
Self-esteem	Self-esteem refers to a person's subjective appraisal of himself or herself as intrinsically positive or negative to some degree.
Individual differences	Individual differences psychology studies the ways in which individual people differ in their behavior. This is distinguished from other aspects of psychology in that although psychology is ostensibly a study of individuals, modern psychologists invariably study groups.
Personality	Personality refers to the pattern of enduring characteristics that differentiates a person, the patterns of behaviors that make each individual unique.
Narcissism	Narcissism is the pattern of thinking and behaving which involves infatuation and obsession with one's self to the exclusion of others.
Empathy	Empathy is the recognition and understanding of the states of mind, including beliefs, desires and particularly emotions of others without injecting your own.
Learning	Learning is a relatively permanent change in behavior that results from experience. Thus, to attribute a behavioral change to learning, the change must be relatively permanent and must result from experience.
Social psychology	Social psychology is the study of the nature and causes of human social behavior, with an emphasis on how people think towards each other and how they relate to each other.
Hypocrisy	Publicly advocating some attitude or behavior and then acting in a way that is inconsistent with this espoused attitude or behavior is called hypocrisy.
Ethnic cleansing	The term ethnic cleansing refers to various policies of forcibly removing people of one ethnic group. At one end of the spectrum, it is virtually indistinguishable from forced emigration and population transfer, while at the other it merges with deportation and genocide.
Self-awareness	Realization that one's existence and functioning are separate from those of other people and things is called self-awareness.
Motives	Needs or desires that energize and direct behavior toward a goal are motives.

Go to **Cram101.com** for the Practice Tests for this Chapter.

Paradigm	Paradigm refers to the set of practices that defines a scientific discipline during a particular period of time. It provides a framework from which to conduct research, it ensures that a certain range of phenomena, those on which the paradigm focuses, are explored thoroughly. Itmay also blind scientists to other, perhaps more fruitful, ways of dealing with their subject matter.
Debriefing	Process of informing a participant after the experiment about the nature of the experiment, clarifying any misunderstanding, and answering any questions that the participant may have concerning the experiment is called debriefing.
Social role	Social role refers to expected behavior patterns associated with particular social positions.
Reasoning	Reasoning is the act of using reason to derive a conclusion from certain premises. There are two main methods to reach a conclusion,deductive reasoning and inductive reasoning.
Bandura	Bandura is best known for his work on social learning theory or Social Cognitivism. His famous Bobo doll experiment illustrated that people learn from observing others.
Obedience	Obedience is the willingness to follow the will of others. Humans have been shown to be surprisingly obedient in the presence of perceived legitimate authority figures, as demonstrated by the Milgram experiment in the 1960s.
Milgram	Milgram conducted the Small world experiment (the source of the six degrees of separation concept) and the experiment on obedience to authority.
Objective self-awareness	Objective self-awareness refers to an organism's capacity to be the object of its own attention, to be aware of its own state of mind, and to know that it knows and remember that it remembers.
Critical thinking	Critical thinking is a mental process of analyzing or evaluating information, particularly statements or propositions that are offered as true.
Social influence	Social influence is when the actions or thoughts of individual(s) are changed by other individual(s). Peer pressure is an example of social influence.
Perception	Perception is the process of acquiring, interpreting, selecting, and organizing sensory information.
Overt behavior	An action or response that is directly observable and measurable is an overt behavior.
Personality trait	According to the Diagnostic and Statistical Manual of the American Psychiatric Association, a personality trait is a "prominent aspect of personality that is exhibited in a wide range of important social and personal contexts. ...".
Agreeableness	Agreeableness, one of the big-five personality traits, reflects individual differences in concern with cooperation and social harmony. It is the degree individuals value getting along with others.
Big five	The big five factors of personality are Openness to experience, Conscientiousness, Extraversion, Agreeableness, and Emotional Stability.
Variable	A variable refers to a measurable factor, characteristic, or attribute of an individual or a system.
Emotion	An emotion is a mental states that arise spontaneously, rather than through conscious effort. They are often accompanied by physiological changes.
Altruism	Altruism is being helpful to other people with little or no interest in being rewarded for one's efforts. This is distinct from merely helping others.
Trait	An enduring personality characteristic that tends to lead to certain behaviors is called a trait. The term trait also means a genetically inherited feature of an organism.

Affect	A subjective feeling or emotional tone often accompanied by bodily expressions noticeable to others is called affect.
Habit	A habit is a response that has become completely separated from its eliciting stimulus. Early learning theorists used the term to describe S-R associations, however not all S-R associations become a habit, rather many are extinguished after reinforcement is withdrawn.
Trait theory	According to trait theory, personality can be broken down into a limited number of traits, which are present in each individual to a greater or lesser degree. This approach is highly compatible with the quantitative psychometric approach to personality testing.
Adaptation	Adaptation is a lowering of sensitivity to a stimulus following prolonged exposure to that stimulus. Behavioral adaptations are special ways a particular organism behaves to survive in its natural habitat.
Empirical	Empirical means the use of working hypotheses which are capable of being disproved using observation or experiment.
Construct validity	The extent to which there is evidence that a test measures a particular hypothetical construct is referred to as construct validity.
Evolution	Commonly used to refer to gradual change, evolution is the change in the frequency of alleles within a population from one generation to the next. This change may be caused by different mechanisms, including natural selection, genetic drift, or changes in population (gene flow).
Moral education	Three types of moral education are character education, values clarification, and cognitive moral education.
Five-factor theory	The five-factor theory of personality proposes that there are five universal dimensions of personality: Neuroticism, Extraversion, Openness, Conscientiousness, and Agreeableness.
American Psychological Association	The American Psychological Association is a professional organization representing psychology in the US. The mission statement is to "advance psychology as a science and profession and as a means of promoting health, education , and human welfare".
Elaboration	The extensiveness of processing at any given level of memory is called elaboration. The use of elaboration changes developmentally. Adolescents are more likely to use elaboration spontaneously than children.
Construct	A generalized concept, such as anxiety or gravity, is a construct.
Wisdom	Wisdom is the ability to make correct judgments and decisions. It is an intangible quality gained through experience. Whether or not something is wise is determined in a pragmatic sense by its popularity, how long it has been around, and its ability to predict against future events.
Empirical evidence	Facts or information based on direct observation or experience are referred to as empirical evidence.
Depression	In everyday language depression refers to any downturn in mood, which may be relatively transitory and perhaps due to something trivial. This is differentiated from Clinical depression which is marked by symptoms that last two weeks or more and are so severe that they interfere with daily living.
Variability	Statistically, variability refers to how much the scores in a distribution spread out, away from the mean.
Heterogeneous	A heterogeneous compound, mixture, or other such object is one that consists of many different items, which are often not easily sorted or separated, though they are clearly distinct.

Narcissist	The narcissist has an unhealthily high self-esteem. For the narcissist, self-worth is the belief that he/she is superior to his/her fellow humans; it is not enough to be "okay" or "pretty good," the narcissist can only feel worthwhile by experiencing him/herself as the "best".
Norms	In testing, standards of test performance that permit the comparison of one person's score on the test to the scores of others who have taken the same test are referred to as norms.
Positive correlation	A relationship between two variables in which both vary in the same direction is called a positive correlation.
Population	Population refers to all members of a well-defined group of organisms, events, or things.
Social psychologists	Social psychologists study the nature and causes of human social behavior, emphasizing on how people think and relate towards each other.
Meta-analysis	In statistics, a meta-analysis combines the results of several studies that address a set of related research hypotheses.
Survey	A method of scientific investigation in which a large sample of people answer questions about their attitudes or behavior is referred to as a survey.
Rape	Rape is a crime where the victim is forced into sexual activity, in particular sexual penetration, against his or her will.
Analogy	An analogy is a comparison between two different things, in order to highlight some form of similarity. Analogy is the cognitive process of transferring information from a particular subject to another particular subject.
Correlation	A statistical technique for determining the degree of association between two or more variables is referred to as correlation.
Quantitative	A quantitative property is one that exists in a range of magnitudes, and can therefore be measured. Measurements of any particular quantitative property are expressed as as a specific quantity, referred to as a unit, multiplied by a number.
Encoding	Encoding refers to interpreting; transforming; modifying information so that it can be placed in memory. It is the first stage of information processing.
Brain	The brain controls and coordinates most movement, behavior and homeostatic body functions such as heartbeat, blood pressure, fluid balance and body temperature. Functions of the brain are responsible for cognition, emotion, memory, motor learning and other sorts of learning. The brain is primarily made up of two types of cells: glia and neurons.
Anti-social	Anti-social behavior is lacking in judgement and consideration for others, ranging from careless negligence to deliberately damaging activity, vandalism and graffiti for example.
Experimental psychology	Experimental psychology is an approach to psychology that treats it as one of the natural sciences, and therefore assumes that it is susceptible to the experimental method.
Cognition	The intellectual processes through which information is obtained, transformed, stored, retrieved, and otherwise used is cognition.
Social policy	Social policy is the study of the welfare state, and the range of responses to social need.
Research method	The scope of the research method is to produce some new knowledge. This, in principle, can take three main forms: Exploratory research; Constructive research; and Empirical research.

Go to **Cram101.com** for the Practice Tests for this Chapter.

Prejudice	Prejudice in general, implies coming to a judgment on the subject before learning where the preponderance of the evidence actually lies, or formation of a judgement without direct experience.
Ingroup	An ingroup is a social group towards which an individual feels loyalty and respect, usually due to membership in the group. This loyalty often manifests itself as an ingroup bias.
Discrimination	In Learning theory, discrimination refers the ability to distinguish between a conditioned stimulus and other stimuli. It can be brought about by extensive training or differential reinforcement. In social terms, it is the denial of privileges to a person or a group on the basis of prejudice.
Social psychologists	Social psychologists study the nature and causes of human social behavior, emphasizing on how people think and relate towards each other.
Stereotype	A stereotype is considered to be a group concept, held by one social group about another.They are often used in a negative or prejudicial sense and are frequently used to justify certain discriminatory behaviors. This allows powerful social groups to legitimize and protect their dominant position
Clique	A clique is an informal and restricted social group formed by a number of people who share common. Social roles vary, but two roles commonly associated with a female clique is notably applicable to most - that of the "queen bee" and that of the "outcast".
Society	The social sciences use the term society to mean a group of people that form a semi-closed (or semi-open) social system, in which most interactions are with other individuals belonging to the group.
Attention	Attention is the cognitive process of selectively concentrating on one thing while ignoring other things. Psychologists have labeled three types of attention: sustained attention, selective attention, and divided attention.
Sexual orientation	Sexual orientation refers to the sex or gender of people who are the focus of a person's amorous or erotic desires, fantasies, and spontaneous feelings, the gender(s) toward which one is primarily "oriented".
Ethnic group	An ethnic group is a culture or subculture whose members are readily distinguishable by outsiders based on traits originating from a common racial, national, linguistic, or religious source. Members of an ethnic group are often presumed to be culturally or biologically similar, although this is not in fact necessarily the case.
Social norm	A social norm, is a rule that is socially enforced. In social situations, such as meetings, they are unwritten and often unstated rules that govern individuals' behavior. A social norm is most evident when not followed or broken.
Perception	Perception is the process of acquiring, interpreting, selecting, and organizing sensory information.
Homosexual	Homosexual refers to a sexual orientation characterized by aesthetic attraction, romantic love, and sexual desire exclusively for members of the same sex or gender identity.
Anxiety	Anxiety is a complex combination of the feeling of fear, apprehension and worry often accompanied by physical sensations such as palpitations, chest pain and/or shortness of breath.
Stereotype threat	A stereotype threat is perceived by persons who believe that they will be evaluated in terms of stereotypes. This is a potential influence on test performance, the resulting anxiety that one's behavior might confirm a negative stereotype about one's group.
Norms	In testing, standards of test performance that permit the comparison of one person's score on

	the test to the scores of others who have taken the same test are referred to as norms.
Friendship	The essentials of friendship are reciprocity and commitment between individuals who see themselves more or less as equals. Interaction between friends rests on a more equal power base than the interaction between children and adults.
Population	Population refers to all members of a well-defined group of organisms, events, or things.
Social psychology	Social psychology is the study of the nature and causes of human social behavior, with an emphasis on how people think towards each other and how they relate to each other.
Affective	Affective is the way people react emotionally, their ability to feel another living thing's pain or joy.
Automaticity	The ability to process information with little or no effort is referred to as automaticity.
Brain imaging	Brain imaging is a fairly recent discipline within medicine and neuroscience. Brain imaging falls into two broad categories -- structural imaging and functional imaging.
Amygdala	Located in the brain's medial temporal lobe, the almond-shaped amygdala is believed to play a key role in the emotions. It forms part of the limbic system and is linked to both fear responses and pleasure. Its size is positively correlated with aggressive behavior across species.
Brain	The brain controls and coordinates most movement, behavior and homeostatic body functions such as heartbeat, blood pressure, fluid balance and body temperature. Functions of the brain are responsible for cognition, emotion, memory, motor learning and other sorts of learning. The brain is primarily made up of two types of cells: glia and neurons.
Allport	Allport was a trait theorist. Those traits he believed to predominate a person's personality were called central traits. Traits such that one could be indentifed by the trait, were referred to as cardinal traits. Central traits and cardinal traits are influenced by environmental factors.
Insight	Insight refers to a sudden awareness of the relationships among various elements that had previously appeared to be independent of one another.
Attitude	An enduring mental representation of a person, place, or thing that evokes an emotional response and related behavior is called attitude.
Self-esteem	Self-esteem refers to a person's subjective appraisal of himself or herself as intrinsically positive or negative to some degree.
Motivation	In psychology, motivation is the driving force (desire) behind all actions of an organism.
Individual differences	Individual differences psychology studies the ways in which individual people differ in their behavior. This is distinguished from other aspects of psychology in that although psychology is ostensibly a study of individuals, modern psychologists invariably study groups.
Emotion	An emotion is a mental states that arise spontaneously, rather than through conscious effort. They are often accompanied by physiological changes.
Innate	Innate behavior is not learned or influenced by the environment, rather, it is present or predisposed at birth.
Ambivalent sexism	A form of sexism characterized by attitudes about women that reflect both negative, resentful beliefs and feelings and affectionate, chivalrous, but potentially patronizing beliefs and feelings is referred to as ambivalent sexism.
Ambivalence	The simultaneous holding of strong positive and negative emotional attitudes toward the same situation or person is called ambivalence.

Incentive	An incentive is what is expected once a behavior is performed. An incentive acts as a reinforcer.
Self-fulfilling prophecy	A self-fulfilling prophecy is a prediction that, in being made, actually causes itself to become true.
Ethnocentrism	Ethnocentrism is the tendency to look at the world primarily from the perspective of one's own culture.
Social class	Social class describes the relationships between people in hierarchical societies or cultures. Those with more power usually subordinate those with less power.
Deprivation	Deprivation, is the loss or withholding of normal stimulation, nutrition, comfort, love, and so forth; a condition of lacking. The level of stimulation is less than what is required.
Authoritarian	The term authoritarian is used to describe a style that enforces strong and sometimes oppressive measures against those in its sphere of influence, generally without attempts at gaining their consent.
Trait	An enduring personality characteristic that tends to lead to certain behaviors is called a trait. The term trait also means a genetically inherited feature of an organism.
Evolution	Commonly used to refer to gradual change, evolution is the change in the frequency of alleles within a population from one generation to the next. This change may be caused by different mechanisms, including natural selection, genetic drift, or changes in population (gene flow).
Personality	Personality refers to the pattern of enduring characteristics that differentiates a person, the patterns of behaviors that make each individual unique.
Critical thinking	Critical thinking is a mental process of analyzing or evaluating information, particularly statements or propositions that are offered as true.
Neuroscience	A field that combines the work of psychologists, biologists, biochemists, medical researchers, and others in the study of the structure and function of the nervous system is neuroscience.
Evolutionary theory	Evolutionary theory is concerned with heritable variability rather than behavioral variations. Natural selection requirements: (1) natural variability within a species must exist, (2) only some individual differences are heritable, and (3) natural selection only takes place when there is an interaction between the inborn attributes of organisms and the environment in which they live.
Self-awareness	Realization that one's existence and functioning are separate from those of other people and things is called self-awareness.
Creativity	Creativity is the ability to think about something in novel and unusual ways and come up with unique solutions to problems. It involves divergent thinking, having many solutions or views to a problem.
Depression	In everyday language depression refers to any downturn in mood, which may be relatively transitory and perhaps due to something trivial. This is differentiated from Clinical depression which is marked by symptoms that last two weeks or more and are so severe that they interfere with daily living.
Consciousness	The awareness of the sensations, thoughts, and feelings being experienced at a given moment is called consciousness.
Kierkegaard	Kierkegaard has achieved general recognition as the first existentialist philosopher, though some new research shows this may be a more difficult connection than previously thought.
World-view	World-view is a term calqued from the German word Weltanschauung meaning a look onto the

world. It refers to the framework through which an individual interprets the world and interacts in it.

Validity	The extent to which a test measures what it is intended to measure is called validity.
Empirical	Empirical means the use of working hypotheses which are capable of being disproved using observation or experiment.
Feedback	Feedback refers to information returned to a person about the effects a response has had.
Affect	A subjective feeling or emotional tone often accompanied by bodily expressions noticeable to others is called affect.
Control subjects	Control subjects are participants in an experiment who do not receive the treatment effect but for whom all other conditions are held comparable to those of experimental subjects.
Paradigm	Paradigm refers to the set of practices that defines a scientific discipline during a particular period of time. It provides a framework from which to conduct research, it ensures that a certain range of phenomena, those on which the paradigm focuses, are explored thoroughly. Itmay also blind scientists to other, perhaps more fruitful, ways of dealing with their subject matter.
Hypothesis	A specific statement about behavior or mental processes that is testable through research is a hypothesis.
Reasoning	Reasoning is the act of using reason to derive a conclusion from certain premises. There are two main methods to reach a conclusion,deductive reasoning and inductive reasoning.
Icon	A mental representation of a visual stimulus that is held briefly in sensory memory is called icon.
Control group	A group that does not receive the treatment effect in an experiment is referred to as the control group or sometimes as the comparison group.
McGregor	McGregor, whose 1960 book The Human Side of Enterprise had a profound influence on management practices, identified an approach of creating an environment within which employees are motivated, which he called theory X and theory Y.
Otto Rank	Otto Rank extended psychoanalytic theory to the study of legend, myth, art, and other works of creativity. He favored a more egalitarian relationship with patients and is sometimes considered the forerunner of client-centered therapy.
Motives	Needs or desires that energize and direct behavior toward a goal are motives.
Variable	A variable refers to a measurable factor, characteristic, or attribute of an individual or a system.
Self-worth	In psychology, self-esteem or self-worth refers to a person's subjective appraisal of himself or herself as intrinsically positive or negative to some degree.
Homophobia	An intense, irrational hostility toward or fear of homosexuals is referred to as homophobia.
Homosexuality	Homosexuality refers to a sexual orientation characterized by aesthetic attraction, romantic love, and sexual desire exclusively for members of the same sex or gender identity.
Lesbian	A lesbian is a homosexual woman. They are women who are sexually and romantically attracted to other women.
Heterosexuality	Sexual attraction and behavior directed to the opposite sex is heterosexuality.
Sexism	Sexism is commonly considered to be discrimination against people based on their sex rather than their individual merits, but can also refer to any and all differentiations based on

Psychopathology	Psychopathology refers to the field concerned with the nature and development of mental disorders.
Bisexuality	Bisexuality is a sexual orientation characterized by aesthetic attraction, romantic love and sexual desire for both males and females.
A priori	The term A Priori is considered to mean propositional knowledge that can be had without, or "prior to", experience.
Questionnaire	A self-report method of data collection or clinical assessment method in which the individual being studied checks off items on a printed list, answers multiple-choice questions, or writes out answers to essay questions aimed at producing a selfdescription is called questionnaire.
Survey	A method of scientific investigation in which a large sample of people answer questions about their attitudes or behavior is referred to as a survey.
Ideology	An ideology can be thought of as a comprehensive vision, as a way of looking at things, as in common sense and several philosophical tendencies, or a set of ideas proposed by the dominant class of a society to all members of this society.
Ethnicity	Ethnicity refers to a characteristic based on cultural heritage, nationality characteristics, race, religion, and language.
Shaping	The concept of reinforcing successive, increasingly accurate approximations to a target behavior is called shaping. The target behavior is broken down into a hierarchy of elemental steps, each step more sophisticated then the last. By successively reinforcing each of the the elemental steps, a form of differential reinforcement, until that step is learned while extinguishing the step below, the target behavior is gradually achieved.
Stages	Stages represent relatively discrete periods of time in which functioning is qualitatively different from functioning at other periods.
Life span	Life span refers to the upper boundary of life, the maximum number of years an individual can live. The maximum life span of human beings is about 120 years of age. Females live an average of 6 years longer than males.
Clinical psychology	Clinical psychology is involved in the diagnosis, assessment, and treatment of patients with mental or behavioral disorders, and conducts research in these various areas.
Tics	Tics are a repeated, impulsive action, almost reflexive in nature, which the person feels powerless to control or avoid.
Anchor	An anchor is a sample of work or performance used to set the specific performance standard for a rubric level .
Conformity	Conformity is the degree to which members of a group will change their behavior, views and attitudes to fit the views of the group. The group can influence members via unconscious processes or via overt social pressure on individuals.
Coding	In senation, coding is the process by which information about the quality and quantity of a stimulus is preserved in the pattern of action potentials sent through sensory neurons to the central nervous system.
Quantitative research	Quantitative research is based on the numerical representation of observations for the purpose of describing and explaining the phenomena. Quantitative research begins with the collection of data, followed by the application of various descriptive and inferential statistical methods.
Signal detection	Signal detection theory is a means to quantify the ability to discern between signal and noise. According to the theory, there are a number of psychological determiners of how we

theory	will detect a signal, and where our threshold levels will be. Experience, expectations, physiological state (e.g, fatigue) and other factors affect thresholds.
Ethnic stereotype	An ethnic stereotype may be either an overly-simplified representation of the typical characteristics of members of an ethnic group or a falsehood that has been repeated so many times that is accepted by many people as generally true.
Chronic	Chronic refers to a relatively long duration, usually more than a few months.
Self-concept	Self-concept refers to domain-specific evaluations of the self where a domain may be academics, athletics, etc.
Premise	A premise is a statement presumed true within the context of a discourse, especially of a logical argument.
Socioeconomic Status	A family's socioeconomic status is based on family income, parental education level, parental occupation, and social status in the community. Those with high status often have more success in preparing their children for school because they have access to a wide range of resources.
Biopsychosocial	The biopsychosocial model is a way of looking at the mind and body of a patient as two important systems that are interlinked. The biopsychosocial model draws a distinction between the actual pathological processes that cause disease, and the patient's perception of their health and the effects on it, called the illness.
Psychosomatic	A psychosomatic illness is one with physical manifestations and perhaps a supposed psychological cause. It is often diagnosed when any known or identifiable physical cause was excluded by medical examination.
Health psychology	The field of psychology that studies the relationships between psychological factors and the prevention and treatment of physical illness is called health psychology.
Psychometric	Psychometric study is concerned with the theory and technique of psychological measurement, which includes the measurement of knowledge, abilities, attitudes, and personality traits. The field is primarily concerned with the study of differences between individuals
Social stigma	A social stigma a distinctive characteristic in a person which can cause or be the result of marginalization when used as an insult by individuals or groups.
Social identity	Social identity is the way we define ourselves in terms of group membership.
Social categorization	Social categorization refers to the tendency to divide the social world into two separate categories: one's in-group and various out-groups.
Overgenerali-ation	Overgeneralization is concluding that all instances of some kind of event will turn out a certain way because one or more in the past did. For instance, a class goes badly one day and I conclude, "I'll never be a good teacher."
Socialization	Social rules and social relations are created, communicated, and changed in verbal and nonverbal ways creating social complexity useful in identifying outsiders and intelligent breeding partners. The process of learning these skills is called socialization.
Self-image	A person's self-image is the mental picture, generally of a kind that is quite resistant to change, that depicts not only details that are potentially available to objective investigation by others, but also items that have been learned by that person about himself or herself.
Sears	Sears focused on the application of the social learning theory (SLT) to socialization processes, and how children internalize the values, attitudes, and behaviors predominant in their culture. He articulated the place of parents in fostering internalization. In addition, he was among the first social learning theorists to officially acknowledge the reciprocal

	interaction on an individual's behavior and their environment
Dissociation	Dissociation is a psychological state or condition in which certain thoughts, emotions, sensations, or memories are separated from the rest.
Cooperative learning	Cooperative learning was proposed in response to traditional curriculum-driven education. In cooperative learning environments, students interact in purposively structured heterogenous group to support the learning of one self and others in the same group.
Jigsaw classroom	The Jigsaw Classroom experiment compared traditional competitive classroom learning with interdependent cooperative learning. Students in the cooperative jigsaw groups demonstrated lower ethnic discrimination, fewer stereotyped attitudes, and higher academic achivement.
Interdependence	Interdependence is a dynamic of being mutually responsible to and dependent on others.
Aronson	Aronson is credited with refining the theory of cognitive dissonance, which posits that when attitudes and behaviors are inconsistent with one another that psychological discomfort results. This discomfort motivates the person experiencing it to either change their behavior or attitude so that consonance is restored.
Superordinate goal	Superordinate goal refers to a goal that exceeds or overrides all others; a goal that renders other goals relatively less important.
Recategorization	Shifts in the boundary between an individual's in-group and an out-group, causing persons formerly viewed as out-group members to now be viewed as belonging to the in-group are called recategorization.
Variability	Statistically, variability refers to how much the scores in a distribution spread out, away from the mean.
Common in-group identity model	The common in-group identity model suggests that to the extent that individuals in different groups view themselves as members of a single social entity, positive contacts between them will increase, and intergroup bias will be reduced.
Superordinate	A hypernym is a word whose extension includes the extension of the word of which it is a hypernym. A word that is more generic or broad than another given word. Another term for a hypernym is a superordinate.
Empathy	Empathy is the recognition and understanding of the states of mind, including beliefs, desires and particularly emotions of others without injecting your own.
Priming	A phenomenon in which exposure to a word or concept later makes it easier to recall related information, even when one has no conscious memory of the word or concept is called priming.
Ethnic identity	An enduring, basic aspect of the self that includes a sense of membership in an ethnic group and the attitudes and feelings related to that membership is called an ethnic identity.
Contact hypothesis	The contact hypothesis suggests that prejudice can be reduced through increased contact among members of different social groups.
Cognition	The intellectual processes through which information is obtained, transformed, stored, retrieved, and otherwise used is cognition.
Meta-analysis	In statistics, a meta-analysis combines the results of several studies that address a set of related research hypotheses.

Social psychology	Social psychology is the study of the nature and causes of human social behavior, with an emphasis on how people think towards each other and how they relate to each other.
Basic research	Basic research has as its primary objective the advancement of knowledge and the theoretical understanding of the relations among variables . It is exploratory and often driven by the researcher's curiosity, interest or hunch.
Applied research	Applied research is done to solve specific, practical questions; its primary aim is not to gain knowledge for its own sake. It can be exploratory but often it is descriptive. It is almost always done on the basis of basic research.
Discrimination	In Learning theory, discrimination refers the ability to distinguish between a conditioned stimulus and other stimuli. It can be brought about by extensive training or differential reinforcement. In social terms, it is the denial of privileges to a person or a group on the basis of prejudice.
Society	The social sciences use the term society to mean a group of people that form a semi-closed (or semi-open) social system, in which most interactions are with other individuals belonging to the group.
Environmental psychology	Environmental psychology is an interdisciplinary field focused on the interplay between humans and their surroundings.
Forensic psychology	Psychological research and theory that deals with the effects of cognitive, affective, and behavioral factors on legal proceedings and the law is a forensic psychology.
Health psychology	The field of psychology that studies the relationships between psychological factors and the prevention and treatment of physical illness is called health psychology.
Epidemiology	Epidemiology is the study of the distribution and determinants of disease and disorders in human populations, and the use of its knowledge to control health problems. Epidemiology is considered the cornerstone methodology in all of public health research, and is highly regarded in evidence-based clinical medicine for identifying risk factors for disease and determining optimal treatment approaches to clinical practice.
Social psychologists	Social psychologists study the nature and causes of human social behavior, emphasizing on how people think and relate towards each other.
Attitude	An enduring mental representation of a person, place, or thing that evokes an emotional response and related behavior is called attitude.
Personality	Personality refers to the pattern of enduring characteristics that differentiates a person, the patterns of behaviors that make each individual unique.
Sleep patterns	The order and timing of daily sleep and waking periods are called sleep patterns.
Perception	Perception is the process of acquiring, interpreting, selecting, and organizing sensory information.
Punishment	Punishment is the addtion of a stimulus that reduces the frequency of a response, or the removal of a stimulus that results in a reduction of the response.
Rape	Rape is a crime where the victim is forced into sexual activity, in particular sexual penetration, against his or her will.
Social support	Social Support is the physical and emotional comfort given by family, friends, co-workers and others. Research has identified three main types of social support: emotional, practical, sharing points of view.
Epidemiological research	The study of the rate and distribution of mental disorders in a population is referred to as epidemiological research.

Cardiovascular disease	Cardiovascular disease refers to afflictions in the mechanisms, including the heart, blood vessels, and their controllers, that are responsible for transporting blood to the body's tissues and organs. Psychological factors may play important roles in such diseases and their treatments.
Immune system	The most important function of the human immune system occurs at the cellular level of the blood and tissues. The lymphatic and blood circulation systems are highways for specialized white blood cells. These cells include B cells, T cells, natural killer cells, and macrophages. All function with the primary objective of recognizing, attacking and destroying bacteria, viruses, cancer cells, and all substances seen as foreign.
Variable	A variable refers to a measurable factor, characteristic, or attribute of an individual or a system.
Population	Population refers to all members of a well-defined group of organisms, events, or things.
Immune response	The body's defensive reaction to invasion by bacteria, viral agents, or other foreign substances is called the immune response.
Tumor	A tumor is an abnormal growth that when located in the brain can either be malignant and directly destroy brain tissue, or be benign and disrupt functioning by increasing intracranial pressure.
Hormone	A hormone is a chemical messenger from one cell (or group of cells) to another. The best known are those produced by endocrine glands, but they are produced by nearly every organ system. The function of hormones is to serve as a signal to the target cells; the action of the hormone is determined by the pattern of secretion and the signal transduction of the receiving tissue.
Catecholamines	Catecholamines are chemical compounds derived from the amino acid tyrosine that act as hormones or neurotransmitters. High catecholamine levels in blood are associated with stress.
Cortisol	Cortisol is a corticosteroid hormone that is involved in the response to stress; it increases blood pressure and blood sugar levels and suppresses the immune system. Synthetic cortisol, also known as hydrocortisone, is used as a drug mainly to fight allergies and inflammation.
Depression	In everyday language depression refers to any downturn in mood, which may be relatively transitory and perhaps due to something trivial. This is differentiated from Clinical depression which is marked by symptoms that last two weeks or more and are so severe that they interfere with daily living.
Cross-sectional design	A research design in which investigators compare groups of subjects of differing age on some variable is a cross-sectional design.
Longitudinal design	A research design in which investigators observe one group of subjects repeatedly over a period of time is called a longitudinal design.
Attention	Attention is the cognitive process of selectively concentrating on one thing while ignoring other things. Psychologists have labeled three types of attention: sustained attention, selective attention, and divided attention.
Stress management	Stress management encompasses techniques intended to equip a person with effective coping mechanisms for dealing with psychological stress.
Psychosomatic	A psychosomatic illness is one with physical manifestations and perhaps a supposed psychological cause. It is often diagnosed when any known or identifiable physical cause was excluded by medical examination.
Etiology	Etiology is the study of causation. The term is used in philosophy, physics and biology in reference to the causes of various phenomena. It is generally the study of why things occur,

Go to **Cram101.com** for the Practice Tests for this Chapter.

or even the reasons behind the way that things act.

Affective	Affective is the way people react emotionally, their ability to feel another living thing's pain or joy.
Psychoneuroi-munology	Psychoneuroimmunology is a specialist field of research that studies the connection between the brain, or mental states, and the immunal and hormonal systems of the human body.
Ischemia	Narrowing of arteries caused by plaque buildup within the arteries is called ischemia.
Coronary heart disease	Coronary heart disease is the end result of the accumulation of atheromatous plaques within the walls of the arteries that supply the myocardium (the muscle of the heart).
Stroke	A stroke occurs when the blood supply to a part of the brain is suddenly interrupted by occlusion, by hemorrhage, or other causes
Regression	Return to a form of behavior characteristic of an earlier stage of development is called regression.
Behavioral medicine	Behavioral medicine refers to an interdisciplinary field that focuses on developing and integrating behavioral and biomedical knowledge to promote health and reduce illness.
Psychosocial treatment	Psychosocial treatment focuses on social and cultural factors as well as psychological influences. These approaches include cognitive, behavioral, and interpersonal methods.
Anatomy	Anatomy is the branch of biology that deals with the structure and organization of living things. It can be divided into animal anatomy (zootomy) and plant anatomy (phytonomy). Major branches of anatomy include comparative anatomy, histology, and human anatomy.
Physiology	The study of the functions and activities of living cells, tissues, and organs and of the physical and chemical phenomena involved is referred to as physiology.
Evolutionary psychology	Evolutionary psychology proposes that cognition and behavior can be better understood in light of evolutionary history.
Hypothesis	A specific statement about behavior or mental processes that is testable through research is a hypothesis.
Physical attractiveness	Physical attractiveness is the perception of an individual as physically beautiful by other people.
Body mass index	The body mass index is a calculated number, used to compare and analyse the health effects of body weight on human bodies of all heights. It is equal to the weight, divided by the square of the height.
Sedentary lifestyle	Sedentary lifestyle is a type of lifestyle common in modern (particularly Western) civilizations, which is characterized by sitting most of the day (for example, in an office or at home). It is believed to be a factor in obesity and other disorders.
Life expectancy	The number of years that will probably be lived by the average person born in a particular year is called life expectancy.
Obesity	The state of being more than 20 percent above the average weight for a person of one's height is called obesity.
Survey	A method of scientific investigation in which a large sample of people answer questions about their attitudes or behavior is referred to as a survey.
Suicide	Suicide behavior is rare in childhood but escalates in adolescence. The suicide rate increases in a linear fashion from adolescence through late adulthood.
Social isolation	Social isolation refers to a type of loneliness that occurs when a person lacks a sense of integrated involvement. Being deprived of participation in a group or community involving

companionship, shared interests, organized activities, and meaningful roles causes a person to feel alone.

Life span	Life span refers to the upper boundary of life, the maximum number of years an individual can live. The maximum life span of human beings is about 120 years of age. Females live an average of 6 years longer than males.
Affect	A subjective feeling or emotional tone often accompanied by bodily expressions noticeable to others is called affect.
Homeostasis	Homeostasis is the property of an open system, especially living organisms, to regulate its internal environment so as to maintain a stable condition, by means of multiple dynamic equilibrium adjustments controlled by interrelated regulation mechanisms.
Brain	The brain controls and coordinates most movement, behavior and homeostatic body functions such as heartbeat, blood pressure, fluid balance and body temperature. Functions of the brain are responsible for cognition, emotion, memory, motor learning and other sorts of learning. The brain is primarily made up of two types of cells: glia and neurons.
Sympathetic	The sympathetic nervous system activates what is often termed the "fight or flight response". It is an automatic regulation system, that is, one that operates without the intervention of conscious thought.
Self-worth	In psychology, self-esteem or self-worth refers to a person's subjective appraisal of himself or herself as intrinsically positive or negative to some degree.
Chronic	Chronic refers to a relatively long duration, usually more than a few months.
Feedback	Feedback refers to information returned to a person about the effects a response has had.
Hypertension	Hypertension is a medical condition where the blood pressure in the arteries is chronically elevated. Persistent hypertension is one of the risk factors for strokes, heart attacks, heart failure and arterial aneurysm, and is a leading cause of chronic renal failure.
Steroid	A steroid is a lipid characterized by a carbon skeleton with four fused rings. Different steroids vary in the functional groups attached to these rings. Hundreds of distinct steroids have been identified in plants and animals. Their most important role in most living systems is as hormones.
Transduction	Transduction in the nervous system typically refers to synaptic events wherein an electrical signal, known as an action potential, is converted into a chemical one via the release of neurotransmitters. Conversely, in sensory transduction a chemical or physical stimulus is transduced by sensory receptors into an electrical signal.
Deprivation	Deprivation, is the loss or withholding of normal stimulation, nutrition, comfort, love, and so forth; a condition of lacking. The level of stimulation is less than what is required.
Diathesis	A predisposition toward a disease or abnormality is a diathesis.
Myocardial infarction	Acute myocardial infarction, commonly known as a heart attack, is a serious, sudden heart condition usually characterized by varying degrees of chest pain or discomfort, weakness, sweating, nausea, vomiting, and arrhythmias, sometimes causing loss of consciousness. It occurs when a part of the heart muscle is injured, and this part may die because of sudden total interruption of blood flow to the area.
Autonomic nervous system	A division of the peripheral nervous system, the autonomic nervous system, regulates glands and activities such as heartbeat, respiration, digestion, and dilation of the pupils. It is responsible for homeostasis, maintaining a relatively constant internal environment .
Nervous system	The body's electrochemical communication circuitry, made up of billions of neurons is a nervous system.

Endocrine system	The endocrine system is a control system of ductless endocrine glands that secrete chemical messengers called hormones that circulate within the body via the bloodstream to affect distant organs. It does not include exocrine glands such as salivary glands, sweat glands and glands within the gastrointestinal tract.
Evolutionary perspective	A perspective that focuses on how humans have evolved and adapted behaviors required for survival against various environmental pressures over the long course is called the evolutionary perspective.
Social neuroscience	The study of the relationship between neural and social processes is called social neuroscience.
Trait	An enduring personality characteristic that tends to lead to certain behaviors is called a trait. The term trait also means a genetically inherited feature of an organism.
Modulation	Modulation is the process of varying a carrier signal, typically a sinusoidal signal, in order to use that signal to convey information.
Critical thinking	Critical thinking is a mental process of analyzing or evaluating information, particularly statements or propositions that are offered as true.
Empirical	Empirical means the use of working hypotheses which are capable of being disproved using observation or experiment.
Intuition	Quick, impulsive thought that does not make use of formal logic or clear reasoning is referred to as intuition.
Premise	A premise is a statement presumed true within the context of a discourse, especially of a logical argument.
Prototype	A concept of a category of objects or events that serves as a good example of the category is called a prototype.
Norms	In testing, standards of test performance that permit the comparison of one person's score on the test to the scores of others who have taken the same test are referred to as norms.
Guilt	Guilt describes many concepts related to a negative emotion or condition caused by actions which are believed to be, morally wrong. According to Freud, the avoidance of guilt is the basis for moral behavior.
Reasoning	Reasoning is the act of using reason to derive a conclusion from certain premises. There are two main methods to reach a conclusion, deductive reasoning and inductive reasoning.
Bentham	Bentham was the first to introduce the concept of the pleasure principle: "Nature has placed mankind under the governance of two sovereign masters, pain and pleasure. It is for them alone to point out what we ought to do, as well as to determine what we shall do."
Kant	Kant held that all known objects are phenomena of consciousness and not realities of the mind. But, the known object is not a mere bundle of sensations for it includes unsensational characteristics or manifestation of a priori principles. He insisted that the scientist and the philosopher approached nature with certain implicit principles, and Kant saw his task to be that of finding and making explicit these principles.
Reflection	Reflection is the process of rephrasing or repeating thoughts and feelings expressed, making the person more aware of what they are saying or thinking.
Procedural justice	Procedural justice concerns the fairness of the processes by which decisions are made.
Research method	The scope of the research method is to produce some new knowledge. This, in principle, can take three main forms: Exploratory research; Constructive research; and Empirical research.

Correlation	A statistical technique for determining the degree of association between two or more variables is referred to as correlation.
Reinforcement	In operant conditioning, reinforcement is any change in an environment that (a) occurs after the behavior, (b) seems to make that behavior re-occur more often in the future and (c) that reoccurence of behavior must be the result of the change.
Dissociation	Dissociation is a psychological state or condition in which certain thoughts, emotions, sensations, or memories are separated from the rest.
Standard deviation	In probability and statistics, the standard deviation is the most commonly used measure of statistical dispersion. Simply put, it measures how spread out the values in a data set are.
Learning	Learning is a relatively permanent change in behavior that results from experience. Thus, to attribute a behavioral change to learning, the change must be relatively permanent and must result from experience.
Double-blind	In a double-blind experiment, neither the individuals nor the researchers know who belongs to the control group. Only after all the data are recorded may researchers be permitted to learn which individuals are which. Performing an experiment in double-blind fashion is a way to lessen the influence of prejudices and unintentional physical cues on the results.
Fisher	Fisher was a eugenicist, evolutionary biologist, geneticist and statistician. He has been described as "The greatest of Darwin's successors", and a genius who almost single-handedly created the foundations for modern statistical science inventing the techniques of maximum likelihood and analysis of variance.
Applied psychology	The basic premise of applied psychology is the use of psychological principles and theories to overcome practical problems.
Experimental psychology	Experimental psychology is an approach to psychology that treats it as one of the natural sciences, and therefore assumes that it is susceptible to the experimental method.
Statistics	Statistics is a type of data analysis which practice includes the planning, summarizing, and interpreting of observations of a system possibly followed by predicting or forecasting of future events based on a mathematical model of the system being observed.
Cognition	The intellectual processes through which information is obtained, transformed, stored, retrieved, and otherwise used is cognition.
Meta-analysis	In statistics, a meta-analysis combines the results of several studies that address a set of related research hypotheses.

Printed in the United States
56718LVS00004B/3

9 781428 802971